To my family

You can't go to bed

With a poem in your head;

It will rattle about

Until it gets out.

So you must set it free

For others to see,

And that is just how

This book came to be.

"There's an N on Your Nose" · First edition
Published in 2022 by Well-Spoken Books

ISBN paperback 979-8-9852756-0-5
ISBN hardback 979-8-9852756-1-2

Dennis Canfield and his family live near Chicago, Illinois. He is also the author of the award-winning Christmas story "South Pole Santa", available in paperback, eBook and audio editions.
For information about other books by Dennis Canfield, please visit denniscanfieldbooks.com

Stella Maris Mongodi is an Italian illustrator based in Edinburgh; she specializes in animals, playful scenes and starry skies.
www.stellamarisart.it

THERE'S AN N ON YOUR NOSE

Dennis Canfield

Stella Maris

Did you know

there's an **N**

on your **NOSE**?

Can you touch the **T** on your **TOES**?

Are there **E**s
in your **EARS**
and your **EYES**?

Was the **H**
in your **HAIR**

a surprise?

Can the **A**

on your **ARM**

say "Hello"...

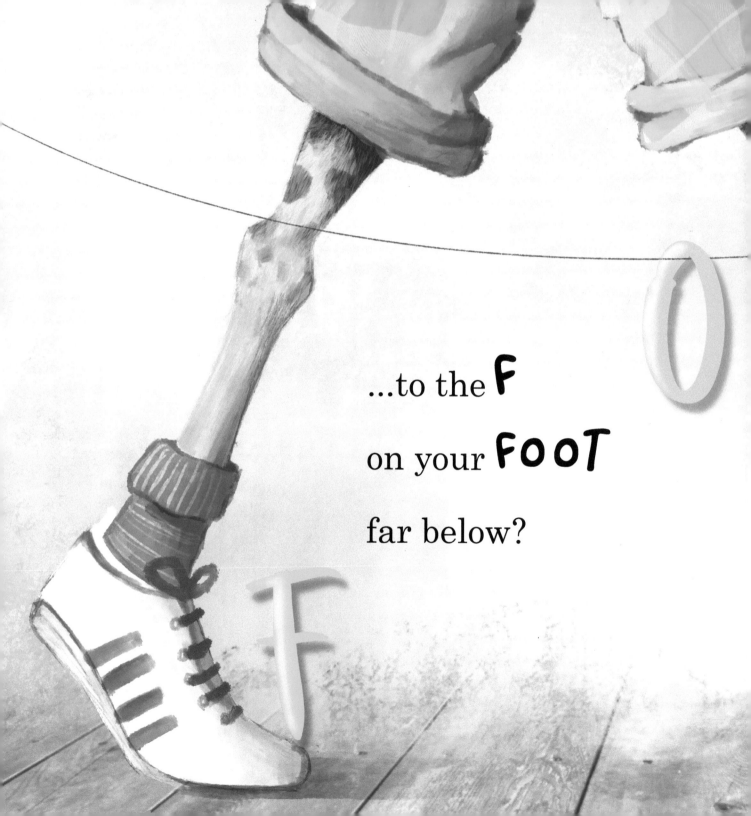

...to the **F**
on your **FOOT**
far below?

Does the **B**
on your **BELLY**

start to giggle...

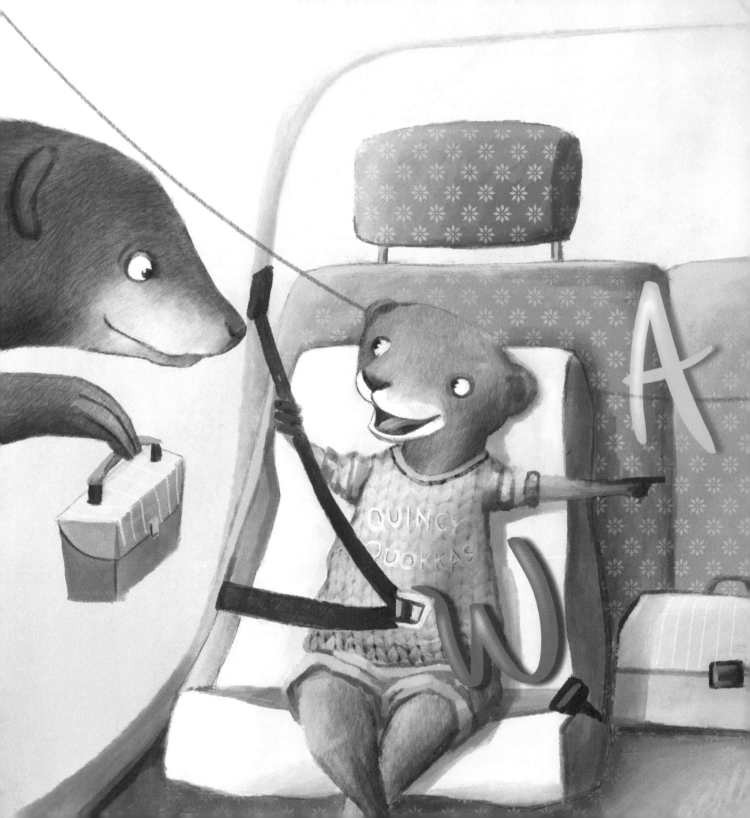

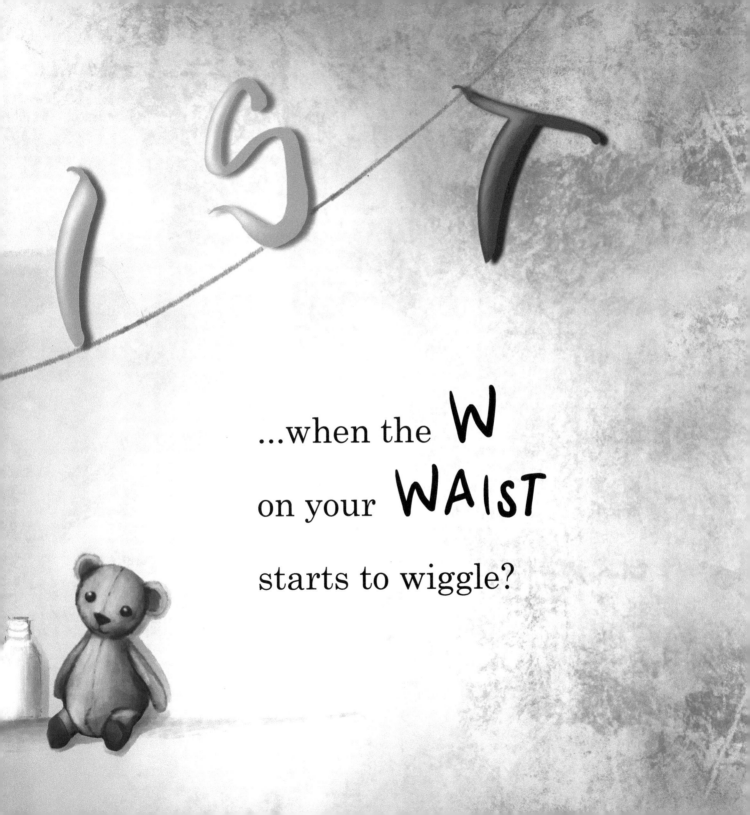

...when the **W**

on your **WAIST**

starts to wiggle?

Could the **L** on your **LIPS** make a grin...

with the **C**s
on your **CHEEKS**
and your **CHIN**?

Did you know...

...there's an **N** on your **NOSE**?

A   B   C   D

I   J   K   L

Q   R   S   T

                Y

E F G H

M N O P

U V W X

Z

CPSIA information can be obtained
at www.ICGtesting.com
Printed in the USA
LVHW071807050722
722707LV00014B/803